Connected  Mathematics™

Data About Us

Statistics

Student Edition

Glenda Lappan
James T. Fey
William M. Fitzgerald
Susan N. Friel
Elizabeth Difanis Phillips

PEARSON

Prentice
Hall

Needham, Massachusetts
Upper Saddle River, New Jersey

The Connected Mathematics Project was developed at Michigan State University with the support of National Science Foundation Grant No. MDR 9150217.

This project was supported, in part,
by the
National Science Foundation
Opinions expressed are those of the authors
and not necessarily those of the Foundation

The Michigan State University authors and administration have agreed that all MSU royalties arising from this publication will be devoted to purposes supported by the Department of Mathematics and the MSU Mathematics Education Enrichment Fund.

Photo Acknowledgements: 6 © John Griffin/The Image Works; 9 © John Whitmer/Stock, Boston; 23 (left) © Rhoda Sidney/The Image Works; 23 (right) © James Fosset/The Image Works; 26 © Ulf Sjostedt/FPG International; 28 © Gale Zucker/Stock, Boston; 30 © Michael Dwyer/Stock, Boston; 53 (top right) © Spencer Grant/Photo Researchers, Inc.; 53 (lower left) © Mike Valeri/FPG International; 53 (lower right) © Lionel Delevingne/Stock, Boston; 59 (left) © Mike Douglas/The Image Works; 59 (right) © Jonathan Meyers/FPG International; 63 © Michael Dwyer/Stock, Boston

Yahtzee is a trademark of the Milton Bradley Company.

ISBN 0-13-180814-1
2 3 4 5 6 7 8 9 10   07 06 05 04 03

The Connected Mathematics Project Staff

Project Directors

James T. Fey
University of Maryland

William M. Fitzgerald
Michigan State University

Susan N. Friel
University of North Carolina at Chapel Hill

Glenda Lappan
Michigan State University

Elizabeth Difanis Phillips
Michigan State University

Project Manager

Kathy Burgis
Michigan State University

Technical Coordinator

Judith Martus Miller
Michigan State University

Curriculum Development Consultants

David Ben-Chaim
Weizmann Institute

Alex Friedlander
Weizmann Institute

Eleanor Geiger
University of Maryland

Jane Mitchell
University of North Carolina at Chapel Hill

Anthony D. Rickard
Alma College

Collaborating Teachers/Writers

Mary K. Bouck
Portland, Michigan

Jaqueline Stewart
Okemos, Michigan

Graduate Assistants

Scott J. Baldridge
Michigan State University

Angie S. Eshelman
Michigan State University

M. Faaiz Gierdien
Michigan State University

Jane M. Keiser
Indiana University

Angela S. Krebs
Michigan State University

James M. Larson
Michigan State University

Ronald Preston
Indiana University

Tat Ming Sze
Michigan State University

Sarah Theule-Lubienski
Michigan State University

Jeffrey J. Wanko
Michigan State University

Evaluation Team

Mark Hoover
Michigan State University

Diane V. Lambdin
Indiana University

Sandra K. Wilcox
Michigan State University

Judith S. Zawojewski
National-Louis University

Teacher/Assessment Team

Kathy Booth
Waverly, Michigan

Anita Clark
Marshall, Michigan

Theodore Gardella
Bloomfield Hills, Michigan

Yvonne Grant
Portland, Michigan

Linda R. Lobue
Vista, California

Suzanne McGrath
Chula Vista, California

Nancy McIntyre
Troy, Michigan

Linda Walker
Tallahassee, Florida

Software Developer

Richard Burgis
East Lansing, Michigan

Development Center Directors

Nicholas Branca
San Diego State University

Dianne Briars
Pittsburgh Public Schools

Frances R. Curcio
New York University

Perry Lanier
Michigan State University

J. Michael Shaughnessy
Portland State University

Charles Vonder Embse
Central Michigan University

Special thanks to the students and teachers at these pilot schools!

Baker Demonstration School
Evanston, Illinois

Bertha Vos Elementary School
Traverse City, Michigan

Blair Elementary School
Traverse City, Michigan

Bloomfield Hills Middle School
Bloomfield Hills, Michigan

Brownell Elementary School
Flint, Michigan

Catlin Gabel School
Portland, Oregon

Cherry Knoll Elementary School
Traverse City, Michigan

Cobb Middle School
Tallahassee, Florida

Courtade Elementary School
Traverse City, Michigan

Duke School for Children
Durham, North Carolina

DeVeaux Junior High School
Toledo, Ohio

East Junior High School
Traverse City, Michigan

Eastern Elementary School
Traverse City, Michigan

Eastlake Elementary School
Chula Vista, California

Eastwood Elementary School
Sturgis, Michigan

Elizabeth City Middle School
Elizabeth City, North Carolina

Franklinton Elementary School
Franklinton, North Carolina

Frick International Studies Academy
Pittsburgh, Pennsylvania

Gundry Elementary School
Flint, Michigan

Hawkins Elementary School
Toledo, Ohio

Hilltop Middle School
Chula Vista, California

Holmes Middle School
Flint, Michigan

Interlochen Elementary School
Traverse City, Michigan

Los Altos Elementary School
San Diego, California

Louis Armstrong Middle School
East Elmhurst, New York

McTigue Junior High School
Toledo, Ohio

National City Middle School
National City, California

Norris Elementary School
Traverse City, Michigan

Northeast Middle School
Minneapolis, Minnesota

Oak Park Elementary School
Traverse City, Michigan

Old Mission Elementary School
Traverse City, Michigan

Old Orchard Elementary School
Toledo, Ohio

Portland Middle School
Portland, Michigan

Reizenstein Middle School
Pittsburgh, Pennsylvania

Sabin Elementary School
Traverse City, Michigan

Shepherd Middle School
Shepherd, Michigan

Sturgis Middle School
Sturgis, Michigan

Terrell Lane Middle School
Louisburg, North Carolina

Tierra del Sol Middle School
Lakeside, California

Traverse Heights Elementary School
Traverse City, Michigan

University Preparatory Academy
Seattle, Washington

Washington Middle School
Vista, California

Waverly East Intermediate School
Lansing, Michigan

Waverly Middle School
Lansing, Michigan

West Junior High School
Traverse City, Michigan

Willow Hill Elementary School
Traverse City, Michigan

Contents

Data About Us

What kinds of information would you like to know about students in your class?

What do we mean when we talk about a "typical" student at your grade level or in your school?

What things could you find out by comparing information about your class with information about other groups of students?

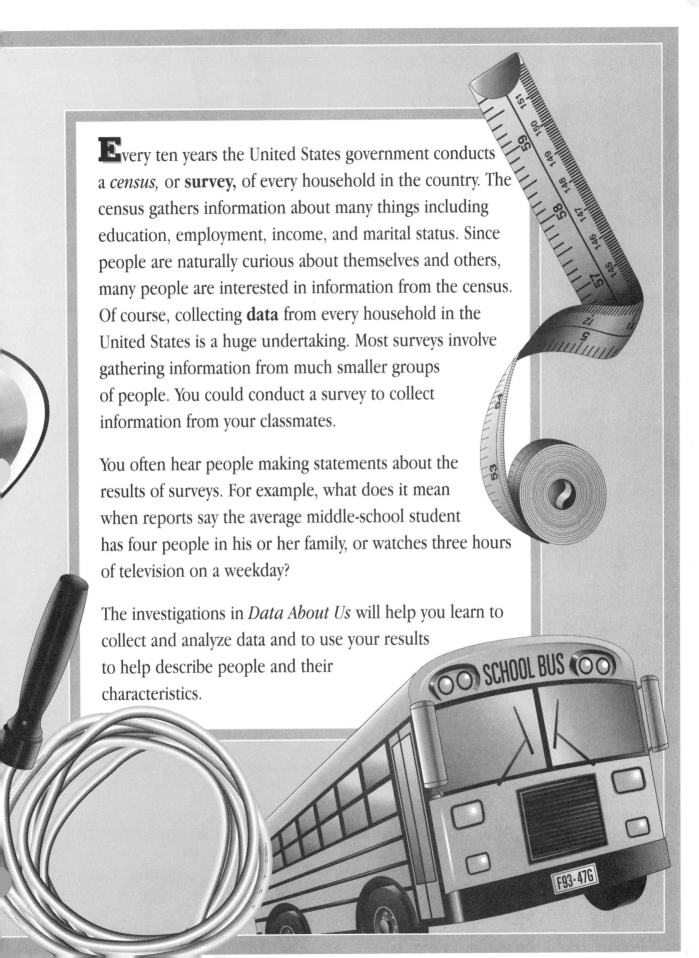

Every ten years the United States government conducts a *census,* or **survey,** of every household in the country. The census gathers information about many things including education, employment, income, and marital status. Since people are naturally curious about themselves and others, many people are interested in information from the census. Of course, collecting **data** from every household in the United States is a huge undertaking. Most surveys involve gathering information from much smaller groups of people. You could conduct a survey to collect information from your classmates.

You often hear people making statements about the results of surveys. For example, what does it mean when reports say the average middle-school student has four people in his or her family, or watches three hours of television on a weekday?

The investigations in *Data About Us* will help you learn to collect and analyze data and to use your results to help describe people and their characteristics.

Mathematical Highlights

In *Data About Us*, you will explore ways of collecting and analyzing data. This unit will help you to

● Understand and use the process of data investigation by posing questions, collecting data, analyzing data, and making interpretations to answer your questions;

● Represent data using line plots, bar graphs, stem-and-leaf plots, and coordinate graphs;

● Compute the mean, median, or mode and the range of a data set;

● Understand the distinctions between categorical data and numerical data and identify which graphs and statistics may be used to represent each kind of data;

● Make informed choices about which graph or graphs and which of the averages (mean, median, mode) and range may be used to describe a data set; and

● Develop strategies for comparing data sets.

As you work on the problems in this unit, ask questions about situations that involve data analysis: *What is the question being asked? How do I want to organize the data set? Which representation is best to use to analyze the data? Do I want to determine an average or the range of the data? If so, which average do I want to use and what will it tell me about the data set? How can I use graphs and statistics to describe a data set or to compare two data sets in order to answer my original question?*

Is Anyone Typical?

What are the characteristics of a typical middle-school student? Who would be interested in knowing these characteristics? Does a typical middle-school student really exist? As you proceed through this unit, you will identify some "typical" facts about your classmates, such as these:

- The typical number of letters in a student's full name
- The typical number of people in a student's household
- The typical height of a student

When you have completed the investigations in *Data About Us,* you will carry out a statistical investigation to answer this question: What are some of the characteristics of a typical middle-school student? These characteristics may include

- physical characteristics (for example, age, height, or eye color)
- family and home characteristics (for example, number of brothers and sisters or number of television sets)
- miscellaneous behaviors (for example, hobbies or number of hours spent watching television)
- preferences, opinions, or attitudes (for example, favorite musical group, or opinions about who should be elected class president)

Keep in mind that a statistical investigation involves posing questions, collecting data, analyzing data, and interpreting the results of the analysis. As you work through each investigation, think about how you might use what you are learning to help you with your project.

Looking at Data

The problems in this investigation involve people's names. Names are filled with symbolism and history. Because family traditions are often involved when a child is named, a person's name may reveal information about his or her ancestors.

Many people have interesting stories about how they were named. Here is one student's story of how her name was chosen: "I'm a twin, and my mom and dad didn't know they were going to have twins. My sister was born first, and she was named Susan. I was a surprise. My mom named me after the woman in the next hospital bed, whose name was Barbara."

Compare stories with your classmates about how you, or someone you know, were named.

1.1 Organizing Your Data

Most parents spend little time worrying about the number of letters in the names they choose for their children. Yet there are times that name length matters. For example, there is sometimes a limit to the number of letters that will fit on a friendship bracelet or a library card.

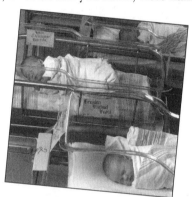

Did you know?

The longest name appearing on a birth certificate is Rhoshandiatellyneshiaunneveshenk Koyaanfsquatsiuty Williams.

Shortly after Rhoshandiatellyneshiaunneveshenk was born, her father filed an amendment that expanded her first name to 1019 letters and her middle name to 36 letters. Can you think of a good nickname for her?

Source: *Guinness Book of World Records*

What do you think is the typical number of letters in the full names (first and last names) of students in your class?

Problem 1.1

Gather data about the total number of letters in the first and last names of students in your class.

A. Find a way to organize the data so you can determine the typical name length.

B. Write some statements about your class data. Note any patterns you see.

C. What would you say is the typical name length for a student in your class?

D. If a new student joined your class today, what would you predict about the length of that student's name?

■ **Problem 1.1 Follow-Up**

Do you think the length of your name is typical for a student in your class? Explain why or why not.

1.2 Interpreting Graphs

A group of students in Ms. Jeckle's class made a **line plot** to display their class's name-length data.

Name Lengths of Ms. Jeckle's Students

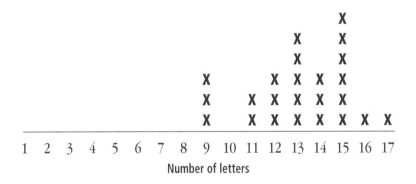

Another group displayed the same data in a bar graph.

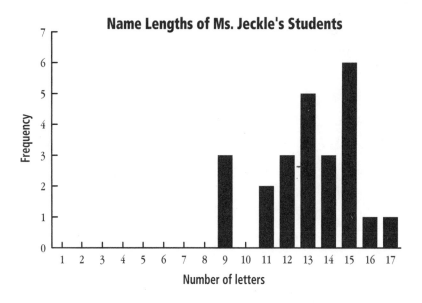

Name Lengths of Ms. Jeckle's Students

Frequency vs. Number of letters

Problem 1.2

Examine the line plot and the **bar graph**.

A. Write some statements about the name lengths for students in Ms. Jeckle's class. Describe any interesting patterns you see in the data.

B. In what ways are the two graphs alike? In what ways are they different?

C. How does the data from Ms. Jeckle's class compare with the data from your class?

■ **Problem 1.2 Follow-Up**

1. How can you use each graph to determine the total number of letters in all the names?

2. Fahimeh Ghomizadeh said, "I have the most letters in my name, but the bar that indicates the number of letters in my name is one of the shortest. Why?" How would you answer this question?

3. Suppose a new student named Nicole Martin joined Ms. Jeckle's class. How could you change the graphs to include data for Nicole?

1.3 Identifying the Mode and Range

One way to describe what is typical, or average, about a set of data is to give the value that occurs most frequently. For example, in the data for Ms. Jeckle's class, the name length 15 occurs most frequently. Six students have 15 letters in their names. Notice that 15 has the highest stack of X's in the line plot and the tallest bar in the bar graph. We call the value that occurs most frequently the **mode** of the data set.

When describing a data set, it is also helpful to give the lowest value and the highest value that occur. The spread of data values from the lowest value to the highest value is called the **range** of the data. In Ms. Jeckle's class, the range of name lengths is from 9 letters to 17 letters.

Think about this!

What are the mode and range of the name-length data for your class? How do the mode and range for your class compare with the mode and range for Ms. Jeckle's class?

Problem 1.3

There are 15 students in a class. The mode of the name lengths for the class is 12 letters, and the range is from 8 letters to 16 letters.

A. Determine a set of name lengths that has this range and mode.

B. Make a line plot to display your data.

C. Use your line plot to help you describe the shape of your data. For example, your data may be bell-shaped, spread out in two or more clusters, or grouped together at one end of the graph.

■ Problem 1.3 Follow-Up

Compare your graph with the graphs some of your classmates drew. How are the graphs alike? How are they different?

Did you know?

Here are some interesting facts about family names.

*   It wasn't until the 1800s that countries in eastern Europe and Scandinavia insisted that people adopt permanent family names.

*   The most common family name in the world is Chang. An estimated 100 million Chinese people have this name.

*   The most common name in the United States, Canada, and the United Kingdom is Smith. There are approximately 2.3 million Smiths in the United States alone.

*   There are over 1.6 million different family names in the United States.

1.4 **Identifying the Median**

You have learned that one way to describe what is typical about a set of data is to give the value that occurs most frequently (the mode). Another way to describe what is typical is to give the middle value of the data set.

The table and line plot below show name-length data for a middle-school class in Michigan. Notice that these data have two modes, 11 and 12. The range of the data is from 8 letters to 19 letters.

Name	Letters
Jeffrey Piersonjones	19
Thomas Petes	11
Clarence Surless	15
Michelle Hughes	14
Shoshana White	13
Deborah Locke	12
Terry Van Bourgondien	19
Maxi Swanson	11
Tonya Stewart	12
Jorge Bastante	13
Richard Mudd	11
Joachim Caruso	13
Roberta Northcott	16
Tony Tung	8
Joshua Klein	11
Janice Vick	10
Bobby King	9
Jacquelyn McCallum	17
Kathleen Boylan	14
Peter Juliano	12
Linora Haynes	12

Class Name Lengths

```
X  X
X  X  X
X  X  X  X                 X
X  X  X  X  X  X  X  X  X  X     X
7  8  9  10 11 12 13 14 15 16 17 18 19 20
```
Number of letters

Cut a strip of 21 squares from a sheet of grid paper. Write the Michigan class's name lengths in order from smallest to largest on the grid paper as shown here.

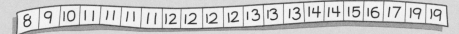

Now, put the ends together and fold the strip in half.

A. Where does the crease land? How many numbers are to the left of the crease? How many numbers are to the right of the crease?

Suppose a new student, Suzanne Mannerstrale, joins the Michigan class. The class now has 22 students. On a strip of 22 squares, list the name lengths, including Suzanne's, in order from smallest to largest. Fold this strip in half.

B. Where is the crease? How many numbers are to the left of the crease? How many numbers are to the right of the crease?

■ Problem 1.4 Follow-Up

The first strip of paper had 21 data values. When you folded the strip, the crease was on the number 12. There were ten values to the left of 12 and ten values to the right of 12. We say that 12 is the *median* of the data set. The **median** of a data set is the value that divides the data in half—half of the values are below the median, and half the values are above the median.

The second strip you made had 22 values. When you folded this strip, the crease landed between 12 and 13. There were eleven values to the left of the crease and eleven values to the right of the crease. When a data set has an even number of values, the median is the value halfway between the two middle values. For this data set, the median is $12\frac{1}{2}$, the number halfway between 12 and 13.

Giving the median of a set of data is one way to describe what is typical about the data. Like the mode, the median is a type of *average*. The median and the mode are sometimes referred to as *measures of center*. You can see that this is a very appropriate description for the median, since it *is* the center of the data.

1. Find the median name length for your class.

2. Use the median, mode, and range to describe what is typical about your class's data.

3. Suppose a student named Chamique Holdsclaw joins your class. Add Chamique's name to your class data, and find the new median. How does the median change?

1.5 Experimenting with the Median

What happens to the median when you add values to or remove values from a set of data? Does adding a value that is much larger or much smaller than the rest of the data values have a greater effect on the median than adding a value that is closer to the other values?

Write each of the names listed below on an index card. On the back of each card, write the number of letters in the name.

Name	Letters
Thomas Petes	11
Michelle Hughes	14
Shoshana White	13
Deborah Locke	12
Tonya Stewart	12
Richard Mudd	11
Tony Tung	8
Janice Vick	10
Bobby King	9
Kathleen Boylan	14

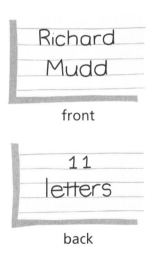

front

back

Order the cards from shortest name to longest name, and find the median of the data.

Problem 1.5

Experiment with your cards to see if you can perform each task described below. Keep a record of the things you try and the discoveries you make.

A. Remove two names without changing the median.

B. Remove two names so the median increases.

C. Remove two names so the median decreases.

D. Add two new names so the median increases.

E. Add two new names so the median decreases.

F. Add two new names without changing the median.

Problem 1.5 Follow-Up

1. If a name with 16 letters were added to the data, what would the new median be?

2. If a name with 1019 letters were added to the data, what would the new median be?

Did you know?

Names from many parts of the world have special origins. European family names were often based on the father's first name. For example, Ian Robertson was the son of Robert, and Janos Ivanovich was the son (vich) of Ivan. Sometimes, the father's first name was used "as is" or with an "s" added to the end. For example, John Peters was the son of Peter, and Henry James was the son of James. Surnames were also created from words that told where a person lived, what a person did, or described personal characteristics. This resulted in names like William Hill, Geoffrey Marsh, Sean Forest, Gilbert Baker, James Tailor, and Kyle Butcher.

Surnames in China and Vietnam often have a long history and are almost always one-syllable words related to names of ruling families. Chang—a name mentioned earlier—is one such example.

Jewish names are sometimes made up of abbreviations that combine a number of words: Katz comes from *kohen tzedek* (righteous priest), and Schatz from *shalian tzibur* (representative of the congregation).

You can read more about names in books such as *Names from Africa* by O. Chuks-orji and *Do People Grow on Family Trees?* by Ira Wolfman.

As you work on these ACE questions, use your calculator whenever you need it.

Applications

For 1 and 2, use the names listed below.

Ben Carter
Ava Baker
Sarah Edwards
Juan Norinda
Ron Weaver
Bryan Wong
Toby Vanhook
Katrina Roberson
Rosita Ramirez
Kimberly Pace
Paula Wheeler
Darnell Cox
Jessica Otto
Erin Froyeh
Corey Buysse
Tijuana Degraffenreid

1. Make a table showing the length of each name. Then make both a line plot and a bar graph of the name lengths.

2. What is the typical name length for this class of students? Use the mode, median, and range to help you answer this question.

In 3–6, use the bar graph below.

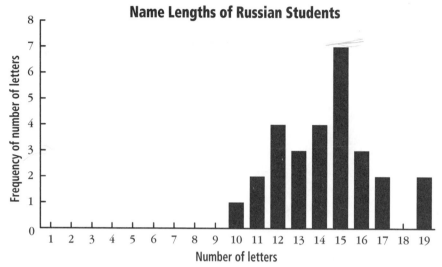

Name Lengths of Russian Students

3. Which value (name length) occurs most frequently? What do we call this value?

4. How many students are in this class? Explain how you got your answer.

5. What is the range of name lengths for this class?

6. What is the median name length? Explain how you got your answer.

For 7–10, make a line plot or bar graph of a set of data that fits the description.

7. 24 names, with a range from 8 letters to 20 letters

8. 7 names, with a median length of 14 letters

9. 13 names, with a range from 8 letters to 17 letters and a median of 13 letters

10. 16 names, with a median of $14\frac{1}{2}$ letters and a range from 11 letters to 20 letters

Connections

In 11–14, use the bar graphs on page 17, which show information about a class of middle-school students.

Graph A

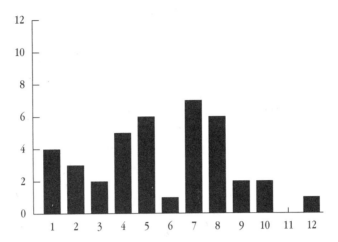

Graph B

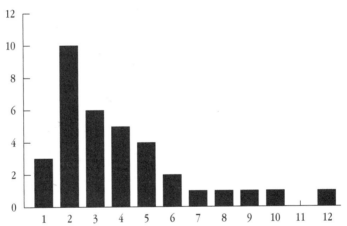

Graph C

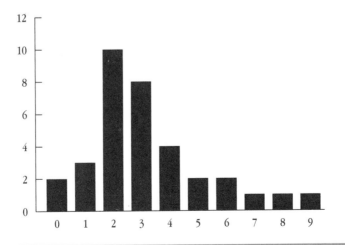

11. Which graph might show the number of children in the students' families? Explain your choice.

12. Which graph might show the birth months of the students? (Hint: Months are often written using numbers instead of names. For example, 1 means January, 2 means February, and 3 means March.) Explain your choice.

13. Which graph might show the number of toppings students like on their pizzas? Explain your choice.

14. Give a possible title, a label for the vertical axis, and a label for the horizontal axis for each graph based on your answers to 11–13.

Extensions

In 15–21, use the table and bar graphs below. A greeting card store sells stickers and street signs with first names on them. The store ordered 12 packages of stickers and 12 street signs for each name. The four bar graphs show the numbers of sticker packages and street signs that remain for the names that begin with the letter A.

Name	Stickers remaining	Street signs remaining
Aaron	1	9
Adam	2	7
Alice	7	4
Allison	2	3
Amanda	0	11
Amber	2	3
Amy	3	3
Andrea	2	4
Andrew	8	6
Andy	3	5
Angela	8	4
Ann	10	7

Graph A:
Stickers Remaining

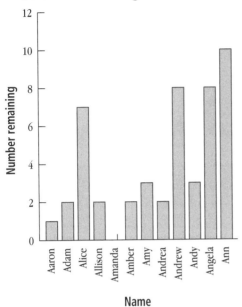

Graph B:
Street Signs Remaining

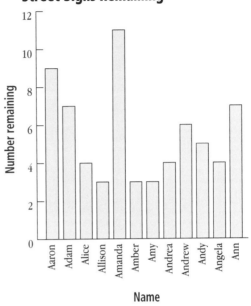

Graph C:
Stickers and Street Signs Remaining

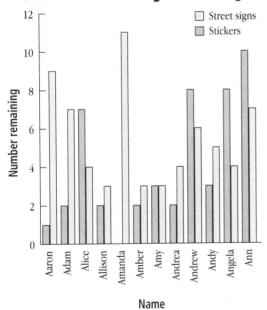

Graph D:
Stickers and Street Signs Remaining

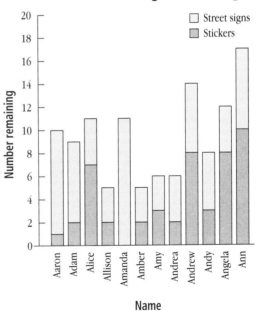

15. In "Graph A" locate the bar that shows the number of stickers left for the name Alice. Explain how you can determine how many stickers are left by reading the graph. Explain how you can determine how many stickers have been sold.

16. In "Graph B" locate the bar that shows the number of street signs left for the name Alice. Explain how you can determine how many street signs are left by reading the graph. Explain how you can determine how many street signs have been sold.

17. Are the stickers more popular than the street signs? Explain your answer.

18. If each package of stickers costs $1.50, how much money has the store made from selling name stickers for names beginning with A?

19. For which name have the most stickers been sold? For which name have the fewest stickers been sold?

20. "Graph C" is a *double bar graph.* Use this graph to determine the name(s) for which the number of street signs sold and the number of sticker packages sold are the same.

21. "Graph D" is a *stacked bar graph.* Use this graph to determine whether some names are more popular than others. Justify your answer.

Mathematical Reflections

In this investigation, you learned some ways to describe what is typical about a set of data. The following questions will help you summarize what you have learned:

1. How are a table of data, a line plot, and a bar graph alike? How are they different?

2. What does the mode tell you about a set of data?

3. What does the median tell you about a set of data?

4. Can the mode and the median for a data set be the same? Can they be different? Explain your answers.

5. Why is it helpful to give the range when you describe a set of data?

6. What does it mean to describe the shape of the data?

7. How can you describe what is typical about a set of data?

Think about your answers to these questions, discuss your ideas with other students and your teacher, and then write a summary of your findings in your journal.

At the end of this unit, you will be developing a survey to gather information about middle-school students. Think of a question or two you might ask. How would you display the information you might gather about each of these questions? Write your thoughts in your journal.

Types of Data

When we are interested in finding out more about something, we start asking questions about it. Some questions have answers that are words or categories, for example, What is your favorite sport? Other questions have answers that are numbers, for example, How many inches tall are you?

Read each of the questions below. Which questions have words or categories as answers? Which questions have numbers as answers?

- In what month were you born?
- What kinds of pets do you have?
- How many pets do you have?
- Who is your favorite author?
- How much time do you spend watching television in a day?
- What's your highest score in the game Yahtzee?
- What color are your eyes?
- How many movies have you watched in the last week?
- How do you get to school?

2.1 Category and Number Questions

The data you collect in response to a question you ask may be numbers or words.

Data that are words or categories are called **categorical data.** Categorical data are usually not numbers. If you asked people in which month they were born or what kinds of pets they have, their answers would be categorical data.

Data that are numbers are called **numerical data.** If you asked people how tall they are or how many pets they have, their responses would be numerical data.

Problem 2.1

Think of some things you would like to know more about. Then, develop some questions you could ask to gather information about those things.

A. Write two questions that have categorical data as answers.

B. Write two questions that have numerical data as answers.

■ Problem 2.1 Follow-Up

Is it possible to find the mode of a set of categorical data? Explain your answer.

2.2 Counting Pets

The pets people have often depend on where they live. People who live in cities often have small pets, while people who live on farms often have large pets. People who live in apartments are sometimes not permitted to have pets at all.

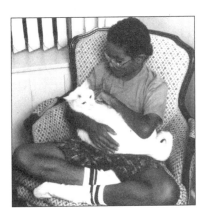 

It is fun to find out what kinds of pets people have. One middle-school class gathered data about their pets by tallying students' responses to these questions:

What is your favorite kind of pet?

How many pets do you have?

The students' questions produced two kinds of data. When students told what their favorite pets were, their responses were categorical data. When students told how many pets they had, their responses were numerical data.

The students made tables to show the tallies or frequencies, and then made bar graphs to display the data.

Favorite Kinds of Pets

Pet	Frequency
cat	4
dog	7
fish	2
bird	2
horse	3
goat	1
cow	2
rabbit	3
duck	1
pig	1

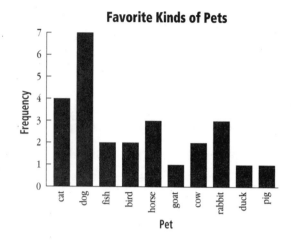

Numbers of Pets

Number of pets	Frequency
0	2
1	2
2	5
3	4
4	1
5	2
6	3
7	0
8	1
9	1
10	0
11	0
12	1
13	0
14	1
15	0
16	0
17	1
18	0
19	1
20	0
21	1

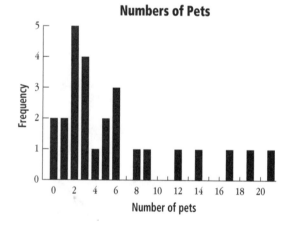

Problem 2.2

Decide whether each question below can be answered by using data from the graphs the students created. If a question can be answered, give the answer and explain how you got it. If a question cannot be answered, explain why not and tell what additional information you would need to answer the question.

A. Which graph shows categorical data, and which graph shows numerical data?

B. What is the total number of pets the students have?

C. What is the greatest number of pets that any student in the class has?

D. How many students are in the class?

E. How many students chose cats as their favorite kind of pet?

F. How many cats do students have as pets?

G. What is the mode for the favorite kind of pet?

H. What is the median number of pets students have?

I. What is the range of the numbers of pets students have?

J. Tomas is a student in this class. How many pets does he have?

K. Do the girls have more pets than the boys?

Problem 2.2 Follow-Up

Do you think the students surveyed live in a city, the suburbs, or the country? Explain your answer.

As you work on these ACE questions, use your calculator whenever you need it.

Applications

In 1–8, tell whether the answers to the question are numerical or categorical data.

1. What is your height in centimeters?

2. What is your favorite musical group?

3. On a scale of 1 to 7, with 7 being outstanding and 1 being poor, how would you rate the food served in the school cafeteria?

4. What would you like to do when you graduate from high school?

5. Are students in Mr. P's class older in months than students in Ms. J's class?

6. How many of your own feet tall are you?

7. What kind(s) of transportation do you use to get to school?

8. How much time do you spend doing homework?

Connections

9. Alicia has a rat that is three years old. She wonders if her rat is old compared to other rats. At the pet store, she finds out that the median age for a rat is $2\frac{1}{2}$ years.

a. What does the median tell Alicia about the life span for a rat?

b. What additional information would help Alicia predict the life span of her rat?

In 10–13, use the graph below, which shows the numbers of sodas consumed by 100 middle-school students in one day.

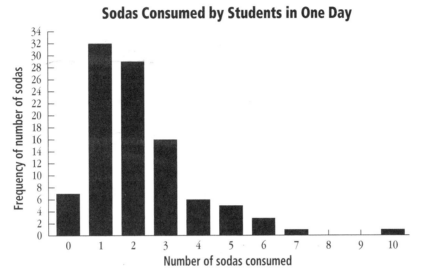

Sodas Consumed by Students in One Day

10. Are these data numerical or categorical? Explain your answer.

11. A student used this graph to estimate that the median number of sodas drunk by these students in a day was 5. Is this student correct? Explain your answer.

12. Another student estimated that the median number of sodas drunk in a day was 1. Is this student correct? Explain your answer.

13. What is the total number of sodas drunk by the 100 students in one day? Describe how you determined your answer.

14. Suppose these students were asked, What kinds of soda do you like to drink?

    a. Give three possible responses to this question.

    b. Describe how you would make a bar graph to show the data that would be collected to answer this question. What would the label for the horizontal axis be? What would the label for the vertical axis be? What would the title of the graph be? What would each bar on the graph show?

Extensions

In 15–17, use the data below. These data were collected from a large number of middle-school students and show the kinds of pets the students have. Of a total of 841 pets, the table shows that 61 are birds and 184 are cats. From this data we cannot tell how many students were surveyed. We only know that when the survey was completed, a total of 841 pets had been counted.

Kinds of Pets Students Have

Kind of pet	Frequency of kind of pet
bird	61
cat	184
dog	180
fish	303
gerbil	17
guinea pig	12
hamster	32
horse	28
rabbit	2
snake	9
turtle	13
Total	**841**

15. Make a bar graph to display this data. Think about how you will design and label the horizontal and vertical axes.

16. Use the information displayed in your graph to write a paragraph about the pets these students have.

17. What might be a good estimate of how many students were surveyed? Explain your reasoning.

Mathematical Reflections

In this investigation, you explored different kinds of data. These questions will help you summarize what you have learned:

1. How would you explain what categorical and numerical data are to a classmate who missed this investigation?

2. You have learned to use the mode and median to describe what is typical about a set of data. Can the mode or median be used to describe categorical data? Can the mode or median be used to describe numerical data?

3. The range is used to help describe how spread out a set of data are. Can you use the range to describe categorical data? Can you use the range to describe numerical data?

Think about your answers to these questions, discuss your ideas with other students and your teacher, and then write a summary of your findings in your journal.

To carry out a research project about characteristics of the typical middle-school student, you will need to pose questions. What questions might you ask that would have categorical data as answers? What questions might you ask that have numerical data as answers?

Using Graphs to Group Data

The data you have seen so far have had small ranges. For example, the name lengths in Problem 1.2 ranged from 9 to 17 letters, and the numbers of pets in Problem 2.2 ranged from 0 to 21 pets. You could see the shape of these data by examining a bar graph or a line plot. For data with a large range, a bar graph or a line plot, with a bar or stack of Xs for every value, often does not give a good idea of the shape of the data. In this investigation, you will learn about a type of graph that groups data values into intervals, making it easier to see the shape of the data.

3.1 Traveling to School

While investigating the times they got up in the morning, a middle-school class in Wisconsin was surprised to find that two students got up almost an hour earlier than their classmates. These students said they got up early because it took them so long to get to school. The class then wondered how much time it took each student to travel to school in the morning. The data they collected are on the next page.

Notice that the data about distances are recorded in decimal form: 4.50 miles means the same thing as $4\frac{1}{2}$ miles. What fractions would you write for 0.75 miles and 2.25 miles?

Think about this!

Look at the table of data and the labels for the columns, and consider these questions.
- What three questions did the students ask?
- How might the students have collected the data to answer these questions?
- Would a line plot be a good way to show the travel-time data? Why or why not?

Student's initials	Time (minutes)	Distance (miles)	Mode of travel
DB	60	4.50	bus
DD	15	2.00	bus
CC	30	2.00	bus
SE	15	0.75	car
AE	15	1.00	bus
FH	35	2.50	bus
CL	15	1.00	bus
LM	22	2.00	bus
QN	25	1.50	bus
MP	20	1.50	bus
AP	25	1.25	bus
AP	19	2.25	bus
HCP	15	1.50	bus
KR	8	0.25	walking
NS	8	1.25	car
LS	5	0.50	bus
AT	20	2.75	bus
JW	15	1.50	bus
DW	17	2.50	bus
SW	15	2.00	car
NW	10	0.50	walking
JW	20	0.50	walking
CW	15	2.25	bus
BA	30	3.00	bus
JB	20	2.50	bus
AB	50	4.00	bus
BB	30	4.75	bus
MB	20	2.00	bus
RC	10	1.25	bus
CD	5	0.25	walking
ME	5	0.50	bus
CF	20	1.75	bus
KG	15	1.75	bus
TH	11	1.50	bus
EL	6	1.00	car
KLD	35	0.75	bus
MN	17	4.50	bus
JO	10	3.00	car
RP	21	1.50	bus
ER	10	1.00	bus

The students decided to make a *stem-and-leaf plot* of the travel times.

Making a Stem-and-Leaf Plot

A **stem-and-leaf plot** looks something like a stem with leaves. It is sometimes simply called a *stem plot*.

To make a stem plot, begin by looking at the data values. Ignore the ones digits and look at the remaining digits of the numbers. These digits will make up the "stem." For these data, the stem will be made up of the tens digits. Since the travel times range from 5 minutes to 60 minutes, the stem will be made up of the digits 0, 1, 2, 3, 4, 5, and 6. Make a vertical list of the tens digits in order from smallest to largest, and draw a line to the right of the digits to separate the stem from the "leaves."

```
0 |
1 |
2 |
3 |
4 |
5 |
6 |
```

The "leaves" are the ones digits. For each data value, you add a leaf next to the appropriate tens digit on the stem. For example, the first data value is 60 minutes. You show this by writing a 0 next to the stem value of 6. The next value is 15 minutes. Indicate this by writing a 5 next to the stem value of 1.

```
0 |
1 | 5
2 |
3 |
4 |
5 |
6 | 0
```

The next few travel times are 30 minutes, 15 minutes, 15 minutes, 35 minutes, 15 minutes, 22 minutes, 25 minutes, and 20 minutes. Can you figure out how these data were added as leaves to the stem plot?

```
0 |
1 | 5 5 5 5
2 | 2 5 0
3 | 0 5
4 |
5 |
6 | 0
```

Copy and complete the stem plot, and compare it to the one below.

```
0 | 8 8 5 5 5 6
1 | 5 5 5 5 9 5 5 7 5 0 5 0 5 1 7 0 0
2 | 2 5 0 5 0 0 0 0 0 1
3 | 0 5 0 0 5
4 |
5 | 0
6 | 0
```

After you have added leaves for all the data values, redraw the plot, listing the ones digits in order from smallest to largest. Then, add a key showing how to read the plot and give the plot a title. Compare your new stem plot to the one below.

Travel Times to School (minutes)

```
0 | 5 5 5 6 8 8
1 | 0 0 0 0 1 5 5 5 5 5 5 5 5 7 7 9
2 | 0 0 0 0 0 0 1 2 5 5
3 | 0 0 0 5 5
4 |
5 | 0
6 | 0
```

Key

2 | 5 means 25 minutes.

Problem 3.1

Read "Making a Stem-and-Leaf Plot" to explore how to make a stem-and-leaf plot of the travel-time data. After you have completed your stem plot of the data, answer these questions.

A. Which students probably get to sleep the latest in the morning? Why do you think this?

B. Which students probably get up earliest? Why do you think this?

C. What is the typical time it takes for these students to travel to school?

■ Problem 3.1 Follow-Up

Consider this question: What is the typical time it takes for a student in your class to travel to school?

1. Decide what data you need to collect to answer this question. Then, with your classmates, gather the appropriate data.

2. Find a way to organize and display your data.

3. After looking at your data, what would you say is the typical time it takes for a student in your class to travel to school?

3.2 Jumping Rope

While doing a jump-rope activity in gym class, a student in Ms. Rich's class wondered what was the typical number of jumps a middle-school student could make without stopping. The class decided to explore this question by collecting and analyzing data. After a practice turn, each student jumped as many times as possible, while a partner counted the jumps and recorded the total. When Mr. Kocik's class found out about the activity, they wanted to join in too.

The classes made a *back-to-back stem plot* (shown on the next page) to display their data. Look at this plot carefully, and try to figure out how to read it.

When the two classes compared their results, they disagreed about which class did better. Mr. Kocik's class pointed out that the range of their data was much greater. Ms. Rich's class said this was only because they had one person who jumped many more times than anybody else. They claimed that most of the students in their class jumped more times than most of the students in Mr. Kocik's class. Mr. Kocik's class disagreed, saying that, even if they did not count the person with 300 jumps, they still did better.

Numbers of Jumps

Ms. R's class		Mr. K's class
8 7 7 7 5 1 1	0	1 1 2 3 4 5 8 8
6 1 1	1	0 7
9 7 6 3 0 0	2	3 7 8
5 3	3	0 3 5
5 0	4	2 7 8
	5	0 2 3
2	6	0 8
	7	
9 8 0	8	
6 3 1	9	
	10	2 4
3	11	
	12	
	13	
	14	
	15	1
	16	0 0
	17	
	18	
	19	
	20	
	21	
	22	
	23	
	24	
	25	
	26	
	27	
	28	
	29	
	30	0

Key

7 | 3 | 0   means 37 jumps for
Ms. R's class and
30 jumps for Mr. K's class.

Which class did better overall in the jump-rope activity? Use what you know about statistics to help you justify your answer.

Problem 3.2 Follow-Up

In Mr. Kocik's class, there are some very large numbers of jumps. For example, one student jumped 151 times, and another student jumped 300 times. We call these data *outliers.* **Outliers** are values that stand out in a set of data.

1. Find two other outliers in the data for Mr. Kocik's class.

Statisticians question outliers and try to figure out why they might have occurred. An outlier may be a value that was recorded incorrectly, or it may be a signal that something special is happening that you may want to understand.

2. All the values recorded for Mr. Kocik's class are correct. What do you think might account for the few students who were able to jump many more times than their classmates?

In 3–5, use the data you collected in Problem 3.1 Follow-Up about the time it takes for you and your classmates to travel to school.

3. Make a back-to-back stem plot showing your class data and the data from the Wisconsin class that was used in Problem 3.1.

4. How do your data and the Wisconsin data compare?

5. Are there any outliers in either of the two data sets? Explain.

As you work on these ACE questions, use your calculator whenever you need it.

Applications

In 1–4, use this stem-and-leaf plot, which shows the number of minutes it took a class of students to travel to school.

Travel Times to School (minutes)

```
0 | 3  3  5  7  8  9
1 | 0  2  3  5  6  6  8  9
2 | 0  1  3  3  3  5  5  8  8
3 | 0  5
4 | 5
```

Key

2 | 5 means 25 minutes.

1. How many students spent 10 minutes traveling to school?

2. Can you use this plot to determine how many students spent 15 minutes or more traveling to school? Explain why or why not.

3. How many students are there in this class? Describe how you determined your answer.

4. What is the typical time it took for these students to travel to school? Describe how you determined your answer.

In 5–8, use the table below. This table shows the ages, heights, and foot lengths for a group of students.

Students Ages, Heights, and Foot Lengths

Age (months)	Height (cm)	Foot length (cm)
76	126	24
73	117	24
68	112	17
78	123	22
81	117	20
82	122	23
80	130	22
90	127	21
101	127	21
99	124	21
103	130	20
101	134	21
145	172	32
146	163	27
144	158	25
148	164	26
140	152	22
114	135	20
108	135	22
105	147	22
113	138	22
120	141	20
120	146	24
132	147	23
132	155	21
129	141	22
138	161	28
152	156	30
149	157	27
132	150	25

5. Make a stem-and-leaf plot that shows the ages in months of the students, starting with the stem shown here. Notice that the first value in the stem is 6, since there are no values less than 60 months.

```
 6 |
 7 |
 8 |
 9 |
10 |
11 |
12 |
13 |
14 |
15 |
```

6. What ages, in years, does the interval of 80–89 months represent? Explain your answer.

7. What is the median age of these students? Explain how you determined this age.

Connections

8.   **a.** Make a stem plot that shows the heights in centimeters of the students.

   b. Make a line plot of the heights in centimeters of the students.

   c. Which of these plots seems the most appropriate for the data? Why?

   d. Would a bar graph be a good way to show this data? Why or why not?

Extensions

In 9 and 10, use the jump-rope data from Ms. Rich's and Mr. Kocik's classes, which are shown on the next page.

Number of Jumps

Mrs. R's Class Data		Mr. K's Class Data	
boy	5	boy	1
boy	35	boy	30
girl	91	boy	28
boy	62	boy	10
girl	96	girl	27
girl	23	girl	102
boy	16	boy	47
boy	1	boy	8
boy	8	girl	160
boy	11	girl	23
girl	93	boy	17
girl	27	boy	2
girl	88	girl	68
boy	26	boy	50
boy	7	girl	151
boy	7	boy	60
boy	1	boy	5
boy	40	girl	52
boy	7	girl	4
boy	20	girl	35
girl	20	boy	160
girl	89	boy	1
boy	29	boy	3
boy	11	boy	8
boy	113	girl	48
boy	33	boy	42
girl	45	boy	33
girl	80	girl	300
		girl	104
		girl	53

9. Make a back-to-back stem-and-leaf plot that compares the girls in Ms. Rich's class with the girls in Mr. Kocik's class *or* the boys in Ms. Rich's class with the boys in Mr. Kocik's class. Did one class of girls (or boys) do better than the other class of girls (or boys)? Explain your reasoning.

10. Make a back-to-back stem-and-leaf plot that compares the girls in both classes with the boys in both classes. Did the girls do better in this activity than the boys? Explain your reasoning.

Mathematical Reflections

In this investigation, you learned how to make stem-and-leaf plots as a way to group a set of data so you can inspect its shape. You looked at two different situations: how long it takes for students to travel to school and how many times students can jump rope. These questions will help you summarize what you have learned:

1 Describe how to locate the median and range using a stem plot.

2 Numerical data can be displayed using more than one kind of graph. How do you decide when to use a line plot, a bar graph, or a stem-and-leaf plot?

3 Some data you gather will be categorical data. Can categorical data be displayed using line plots, bar graphs, or stem-and-leaf plots? Explain your reasoning.

Think about your answers to these questions, discuss your ideas with other students and your teacher, and then write a summary of your findings in your journal.

Think about the survey you will be developing to gather information about middle-school students. What kinds of questions can you ask that might involve using a stem-and-leaf plot to display the data?

Coordinate Graphs

In the first three investigations, you worked with one measure at a time. For example, you looked at the number of letters in students' names, the number of times students jumped rope, or the numbers of pets students had. Although you can find out some interesting things about one set of data, it is often interesting to look at how two sets of data are related to each other.

4.1 Relating Height to Arm Span

If you look around at your classmates, you might guess that taller people have wider arm spans. But is there *really* any relationship between a person's height and his or her arm span? The best way to find out more about this question is to collect some data.

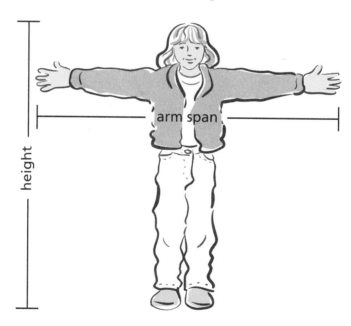

Here are data on height and arm span (measured from fingertip to fingertip) that one class collected.

Height and Arm Span Measurements

Initials	Height (inches)	Arm span (inches)
NY	63	60
JJ	69	67
CM	73	75
PL	77	77
BP	64	65
AS	67	64
KR	72	72

One way to show data about two different measures (such as height and arm span) at the same time is to make a **coordinate graph.** Each point on a coordinate graph represents two measures for one person or thing. On a coordinate graph, the horizontal axis, or *x*-axis, represents one measure. The vertical axis, or *y*-axis, represents a second measure. For example, the graph below shows data for height along the *x*-axis and data for arm span along the *y*-axis. Each point on this graph indicates both the height and the arm span for one student.

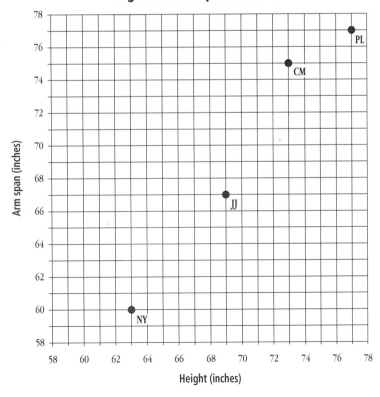

Height and Arm Span Measurements

Study the table of data and the coordinate graph. Four points have already been plotted and labeled with the students' initials. We write the location for each point like this:

- NY is located at point (63, 60)
- JJ is located at point (69, 67)
- CM is located at point (73, 75)
- PL is located at point (77, 77)

Working with a partner, determine how to locate points on this graph. Where would you place the points and initials for the remaining three people? Why do the axes start at (58, 58)? What would the graph look like if the axes started at (0, 0)?

Problem 4.1

Think about this question: If you know the measure of a person's arm span, do you know anything about his or her height?

To help you answer this question, you will need to collect some data. With your class, collect the height and arm span of each person in your class. Make a coordinate graph of your data. Then, use your graph to answer the question above.

■ Problem 4.1 Follow-Up

Draw a diagonal line through the points on the graph where the measures for arm span and height are the same.

1. How many of your classmates' data are on this line? What is true about arm span compared to height for the points on this line?

2. What is true about arm span compared to height for the points *below* the line you drew?

3. What is true about arm span compared to height for the points *above* the line you drew?

4.2 Relating Travel Time to Distance

In Investigation 3, you made stem plots to show data about travel times to school. Using a coordinate graph, you can show both travel time and distance from home to school. For example, we can show the travel time and distance to school for the students in Problem 3.1 on a coordinate graph:

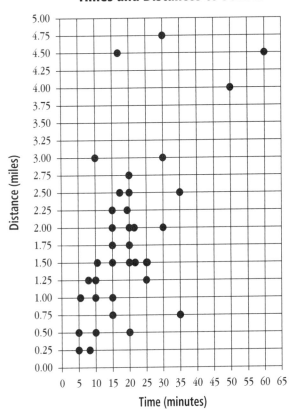

Times and Distances to School

Problem 4.2

Study the graph above, which was made using the data from Problem 3.1.

A. Look back at the data on page 31. On Labsheet 4.2, locate and label with initials the points for the first five students in the table.

B. If you know how long it takes a particular student to travel to school, can you know anything about that student's distance from school? Use the graph to help you answer this question. Write a justification for your answer.

Problem 4.2 Follow-Up

1. Locate the points at (17, 4.50) and (60, 4.50) on the coordinate graph on Labsheet 4.2. What can you tell about the students these points represent?

2. Locate the points (30, 2.00), (30, 3.00), and (30, 4.75). What can you tell about the students these points represent?

3. What would the graph look like if the same scale were used for both axes?

As you work on these ACE questions, use your calculator whenever you need it.

Applications

In 1 and 2, use this table of data, which shows the ages, heights, and foot lengths for 30 students.

Student Age, Height, and Foot Length

Age (months)	Height (cm)	Foot length (cm)
76	126	24
73	117	24
68	112	17
78	123	22
81	117	20
82	122	23
80	130	22
90	127	21
101	127	21
99	124	21
103	130	20
101	134	21
145	172	32
146	163	27
144	158	25
148	164	26
140	152	22
114	135	20
108	135	22
105	147	22
113	138	22
120	141	20
120	146	24
132	147	23
132	155	21
129	141	22
138	161	28
152	156	30
149	157	27
132	150	25

1. a. Make a stem-and-leaf plot showing the heights of these students.

b. Can you determine from your stem plot whether the youngest student is also the shortest? Can you determine this from the table? Explain why or why not.

2. a. On a piece of grid paper, make a coordinate graph showing each person's age (in months) on the horizontal axis and height (in centimeters) on the vertical axis. To help you choose a scale for each axis, look at the range of values you have to locate on the graph. What are the smallest and largest age values? What are the smallest and largest height values?

b. Can you determine from your coordinate graph whether the youngest student is also the shortest student? Explain your reasoning.

c. Using information from your coordinate graph, describe what happens to students' heights as students get older.

d. We know people eventually stop growing. When does this happen? How would this affect the graph?

3. The coordinate graph on the next page displays height and foot length for 29 students. Notice that the x-axis is scaled in intervals of 5 centimeters and the y-axis is scaled in intervals of 1 centimeter.

a. One student said that if you know a person's foot length, you can tell what that person's height is. Do you think she is right? Explain your reasoning.

b. Determine the median height and the median foot length. Compare the median height with the median foot length. The median height is about how many times as large as the median foot length?

c. Measure the length of your foot and your height in centimeters. Your height is about how many times as large as your foot length?

d. Look at your responses to b and c. How can you use this information to decide whether the student's comment in a is correct?

e. What would the graph look like if each axis started at 0?

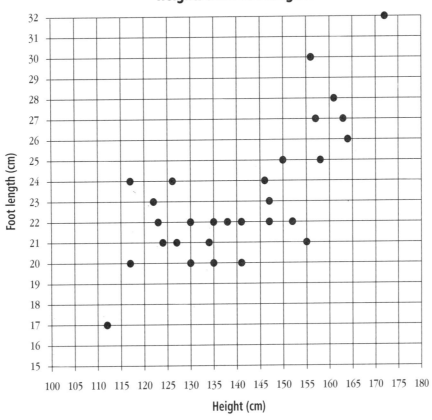

Heights and Foot Lengths

Connections

4. Make a coordinate graph that shows the numbers from 1 to 20 on the horizontal axis and the number of factors of each of these numbers on the vertical axis. What patterns do you see in your graph? Explain each pattern.

Extensions

5. A group of students challenged each other to see who could come the closest to guessing the number of seeds in his or her pumpkin. In October, they guessed the number of seeds in each of their pumpkins. In November, they opened their pumpkins and counted the seeds. They compared their guesses with their actual counts by displaying their data on a coordinate graph. The data and graph are shown on the next page.

a. Describe what you notice about how spread out the actual counts are. What are the median and the range of the actual counts?

b. Describe what you notice about how spread out the guesses are. What are the median and the range of the guesses?

c. On Labsheet 4.ACE, draw a diagonal line on the graph to connect the points (0, 0), (250, 250), (500, 500), all the way to (2250, 2250).

d. What is true about the guesses compared to the actual counts for points on or near the line you drew?

e. What is true about the guesses compared to the actual counts for points above the line?

f. What is true about the guesses compared to the actual counts for points below the line?

g. In general, did the students make good guesses about the numbers of seeds in their pumpkins? Use what you know about the median and range of the actual counts and the guesses as well as other information from the graph to explain your reasoning.

h. The scales on the axes are the same, but the data are very bunched together. How would you change the scale to better show the data points?

Numbers of Seeds
in Pumpkins

Guess	Actual
630	309
621	446
801	381
720	505
1900	387
1423	336
621	325
1200	365
622	410
1000	492
1200	607
1458	498
350	523
621	467
759	423
900	479
500	512
521	606
564	494
655	441
722	455
202	553
621	367
300	442
200	507
556	462
604	384
2000	545
1200	354
766	568
624	506
680	486
605	408
1100	387

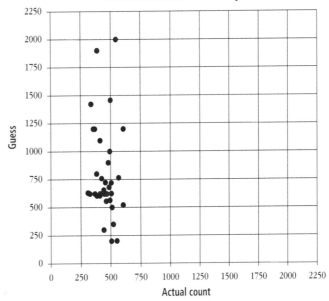

Numbers of Seeds in Pumpkins

Mathematical Reflections

In this investigation, you have learned how to make and read coordinate graphs. Coordinate graphs let you examine two sets of data at once so you can look for relationships between pairs of data. You looked at two different situations: how arm span relates to height, and how travel time relates to distance traveled. These questions will help you summarize what you have learned:

1 When you make a coordinate graph of data pairs, what do you consider when deciding what scale to use on each axis?

2 How do you locate a point on a coordinate graph?

3 If you make a coordinate graph of variables such as arm span and height, where the values of one measure get larger as the values of the other measure get larger, what will the pattern of points on the graph look like?

4 How are a coordinate graph and a line plot alike? How are they different?

Think about your answers to these questions, discuss your ideas with other students and your teacher, and then write a summary of your findings in your journal.

Think about how what you have learned about coordinate graphs might help you with your project. What kinds of questions can you ask to help you answer the question, "Is anyone typical?" that might involve using a coordinate graph to display the data?

What Do We Mean by *Mean?*

Since the first United States census was conducted in 1790, its primary use has been to find out how many people live in the United States. These data, organized by state, are used to determine how many representatives each state will have in the House of Representatives in the United States Congress.

Many people are interested in the census because it provides useful information about a number of other things, including household size. The term *household*, as used by the United States census, means all the people who occupy a "housing unit" (a house, an apartment or other group of rooms, or a single room like a room in a boarding house).

Remember that an *average* is a value used to describe what is typical about a set of data. An average can be thought of as a "measure of center." The mode and the median are two types of averages you have used quite a bit. The *mode* is the value that occurs most frequently in a set of data. The *median* is the value that divides a set of ordered data in half. This investigation explores a third kind of average, which is called the *mean.*

5.1 Evening Things Out

Six students in a middle-school class determined the number of people in their households using the United States census guidelines. Each student then made a cube tower to show the number of people in his or her household.

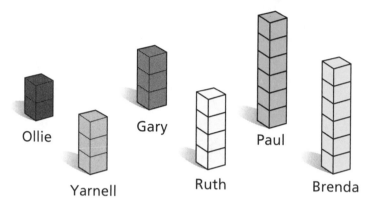

You can easily see from the cube towers that the six households vary in size. The students wondered what the average number of people is in their households. Their teacher asked them what they might do, using their cube towers, to find the answer to their question.

Problem 5.1

What are some ways to determine the average number of people in these six households?

■ Problem 5.1 Follow-Up

The students had an idea for finding the average number of people in the households. They decided to rearrange the cubes to try to "even out" the number of cubes in each tower. Try this on your own and see what you find for the average number of people in the households, and then read on to see what the students did.

First, the students put the towers in order.

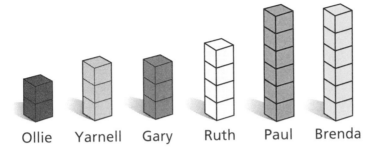

The students then moved cubes from one tower to another, making some households bigger than they actually were and making other households smaller than they actually were. When they were finished moving cubes, their towers looked like this:

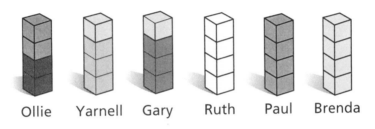

Each tower now had four cubes. Notice that the total number of cubes did not change.

Before	
Ollie	2 people
Yarnell	3 people
Gary	3 people
Ruth	4 people
Paul	6 people
Brenda	6 people
Total	24 people

After	
Ollie	4 people
Yarnell	4 people
Gary	4 people
Ruth	4 people
Paul	4 people
Brenda	4 people
Total	24 people

The students determined that the average number of people in a household was 4. The teacher explained that the average the students had found is called the **mean.** The mean number of people in the six households is 4.

The students decided to look at the data in another way. They used stick-on notes to make a line plot of the data. They used an arrow to show the mean on their line plot.

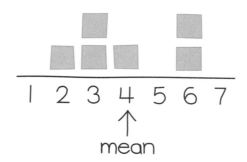

Notice that in the 6 households there is a total of 24 people: $2 + 3 + 3 + 4 + 6 + 6 = 24$. You can see that the mean is not the middle of the distribution since there are 2 households above the mean and 3 households below the mean.

One student said, "When you even out the cubes, it's like moving all the stick-on notes to the same place on the line plot." The students showed this on their line plot.

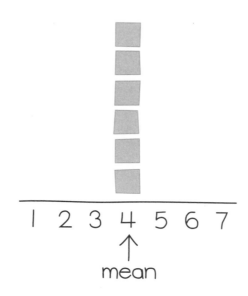

Notice that the total number of people in the households is still 24:
$4 + 4 + 4 + 4 + 4 + 4 = 24$.

The mean is a kind of balance point in the distribution. You can see that the sizes of some households are less than the mean and the sizes of some households are more than the mean. However, there are enough people in the households above the mean that can be moved to the households below the mean so that the households can be "evened out" with 4 people in each.

5.2 Finding the Mean

The following data show the number of people in the households of six different students.

Name	Number of people in household
Geoffrey	6
Betty	4
Brendan	3
Oprah	4
Reilly	3
Tonisha	4

Problem 5.2

A. Make a set of cube towers to show the size of each household.

B. Make a line plot of the data.

C. How many people are there in the six households altogether? Describe how you determined your answer.

D. What is the mean number of people in the six households? Describe how you determined your answer.

■ Problem 5.2 Follow-Up

1. How does the mean for this set of six students compare to the mean for the six students in Problem 5.1?

2. How does the median for this set of six students compare to the median for the six students in Problem 5.1?

5.3 Data with the Same Mean

The line plots below show the data from Problem 5.1 and Problem 5.2. The data for the two situations look different, but the mean is the same.

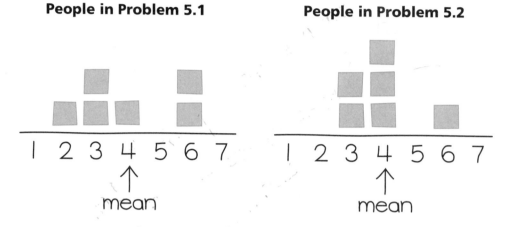

People in Problem 5.1   **People in Problem 5.2**

Think about these questions:
- How many households are there in each situation?
- How many total people are there in each situation?
- How are these facts related to the mean of 4 in each case?

Problem 5.3

A. Try to find two more sets of six households with a mean of 4 people. Use cubes to show each set, and then make line plots that show the information from the cubes.

B. Try to find two different sets of seven households with a mean of 4 people. Use cubes to show each set, and then make line plots to show the information from the cubes.

Problem 5.3 Follow-Up

1. A group of seven students has a mean number of 3 people in their households. Make a line plot showing a data set that fits this description.
2. A group of six students has a mean number of $3\frac{1}{2}$ people in their households. Make a line plot showing a data set that fits this description.
3. How can the mean be $3\frac{1}{2}$ people when "half" people do not exist?

Using Your Class's Data

Recall that the term *household* as used by the United States census refers to all people who occupy a "housing unit" (a house, an apartment or other group of rooms, or a single room like a room in a boarding house).

Problem 5.4

A. Using the definition from the United States census, how many people are in your household?

B. Collect household data from everyone in your class, and make a display to show the information.

C. What is the mean number of people in your class's households? Describe how you determined your answer.

■ Problem 5.4 Follow-Up

One student wrote, "In Problem 5.2, there are 6 households with a total of 24 people. There is a range of 3 to 6 people in the 6 households. The mean number of people in each household is 4. This is the number that tells me how many people each household would have if each household had the same number of people." Write a similar description for your class data about people in your households.

5.5 Watching Movies

A group of middle-school students was asked this question: How many movies did you watch last month? Here are a table and stem plot of the data:

Student	Number of movies
Joel	15
Tonya	16
Rachel	5
Lawrence	18
Meela	3
Leah	6
Beth	7
Mickey	6
Bhavana	3
Josh	11

Movies Watched

```
0 | 3 3 5 6 6 7
1 | 1 5 6 8
2 |
```

Key

1 | 5   means 15 movies.

Problem 5.5

A. Look at the table above and complete these statements.

The total number of students is _____.

The total number of movies watched is _____.

The mean number of movies watched is _____.

B. A new value is added for Lucia, who watched 42 movies last month. This value is an outlier. How does the stem plot change when this value is added? What is the new mean? Compare the mean from part A to the mean after this value is added. What do you notice?

C. A new value is added for Tamara, who was home last month with a broken leg. She watched 96 movies. What is the mean of the data now? Compare the means you found in parts A and B with this new mean. What do you notice? Why?

D. Data for eight more students are added:

Tommy	5	Robbie	4
Alexandra	5	Ana	4
Kesh	5	Alisha	2
Kirsten	5	Brian	2

These data are not outliers, but now there are several students who watched only a few movies in one month. What is the mean of the data now? Compare the means you found in parts A, B, and C with this new mean. What do you notice? Why?

■ Problem 5.5 Follow-Up

1. What happens to the mean when you add one or more values that are much larger than the values in the original data set? Why does this happen?

2. What happens to the mean when you add a number of values that are clumped with the smaller values in the original data set? Why does this happen?

As you work on these ACE questions, use your calculator whenever you need it.

Applications

In 1 and 2, use the line plot below, which shows information about the number of children found in 16 households.

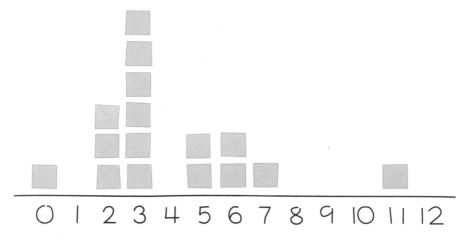

1. **a.** What is the median number of children in the 16 households? Explain how you found the median and what it tells you.

   b. Do any of the 16 households have the median number of children? Explain why this is possible.

2. **a.** What is the mean number of children in the 16 households? Explain how you found the mean and what it tells you.

   b. Do any of the 16 households have the mean number of children? Explain why this is possible.

3. The mean number of people in eight households is 6.

   a. What is the total number of people in the eight households?

   b. Make a line plot showing one possible arrangement for the numbers of people in the eight households.

c. Make a line plot showing a different possible arrangement for the numbers of people in the eight households.

d. Are the medians the same for the two arrangements you made?

4. A group of nine students has a mean of $3\frac{1}{2}$ people in their households. Make a line plot showing an example of this data set.

5. A group of nine students has a mean of 5 people in their households, and the largest household in the group has 10 people. Make a line plot of a data set fitting this description.

Connections

6. Jon has a pet rabbit that is 5 years old. He wonders if his rabbit is old compared to other rabbits. At the pet store, he finds out that the mean age for a rabbit is 7 years.

a. What does the mean tell Jon about the life span for a rabbit?

b. What additional information would help Jon to predict the life span of his rabbit?

7. A store carries nine different brands of granola bars. What are possible prices for each of the nine brands of granola bars if the mean price is $1.33? Explain how you determined the values for each of the nine brands. You may use pictures to help you.

8. Three candidates are running for the mayor of Slugville. Each has determined the typical income for the people in Slugville and is using this information to help in the campaign.

Mayor Phibbs is running for re-election. He says, "Slugville is doing great! The average income for each person is $2000 per week!"

Challenging candidate Louisa Louis says, "Slugville is nice, but it needs my help! The average income is only $100 per week."

Radical Ronnie Radford says, "No way! We must burn down the town—it's awful. The average income is $0 per week."

None of the candidates is lying. Slugville has only 16 residents, and their weekly incomes are $0, $0, $0, $0, $0, $0, $0, $0, $200, $200, $200, $200, $200, $200, $200, and $30,600.

a. Explain how each of the candidates determined what the "average" income was for the town. Check the computations to see whether you agree with the three candidates.

b. Does any person in Slugville have the mean income? Explain.

c. Does any person in Slugville have the median income? Explain.

d. Does any person in Slugville have the mode income? Explain.

e. What do you consider to be the typical income for a resident of Slugville? Explain.

f. If four more people moved to Slugville, each with a weekly income of $200, how would the mean, median, and mode change?

9. A recent survey asked 25 middle-school students how many movies they watch in one month. The data are shown on the next page. Notice that the data are quite spread out; the range is from 1 to 30 movies.

a. Make a stem-and-leaf plot to show these data. Describe the shape of the data.

b. Find the mean number of movies watched by the students for the month.

c. Describe how you found the mean number of movies.

d. What do the mean and the range tell you about the typical number of movies watched for this group of students?

e. Find the median number of movies watched. Are the mean and the median the same? Why do you think this is so?

Movies Watched by Students

Student	Movies per month
Wes	2
Sanford	15
Carla	13
Su Chin	1
Michael	9
Mara	30
Alan	20
Brent	1
Tanisha	25
Susan	4
Darlene	3
Eddie	2
Lonnie	3
Gerald	10
Kristina	15
Paul	12
Henry	5
Julian	2
Greta	4
TJ	1
Rebecca	4
Ramish	11
Art	8
Raymond	8
Angelica	17

Extensions

In 10 and 11, consider this newspaper headline:

10. Which average—median or mean—do you think is being used in this headline? Explain why you think this.

11. About how many hours per day does the average third grader watch television if he or she watches 1170 hours in a year?

12. Review the jump-rope data for Problem 3.2 on page 35.

a. Compute the median and the mean for each class's data. How do the median and the mean for each compare?

b. Which statistic—the median or the mean—would Mr. Kocik's class want to use to compare their performance with Ms. Rich's class? Why?

c. What happens to the median of Mr. Kocik's class's data if you leave out the data for the student who jumped rope 300 times? Why does this happen?

d. What happens to the mean of Mr. Kocik's class's data if you leave out the data for the student who jumped rope 300 times? Why does this happen?

e. Can Ms. Rich's class claim to be better if the data of 300 jumps is left out of Mr. Kocik's class's data? Explain why or why not.

Mathematical Reflections

In this investigation, you explored a type of average called the mean. You used cubes to help you see what it means to "even out" data to locate the mean, and you created different data sets with the same mean. Then you developed a way to find the mean without using cubes. Finally, you looked at what happens to the mean when the data include very high or very low values. These questions will help you summarize what you have learned:

1 Describe a method that requires using only numbers for finding the mean. Explain why this method works.

2 You have used three measures of center: the mode, the median, and the mean.

    a. Why do you suppose these are called "measures of center"? What does each tell you about a set of data?

    b. Why might people prefer to use the median instead of the mean?

3 You have used one measure of spread: the range.

    a. Why do you suppose the range is called a "measure of spread"?

    b. Why might people prefer to describe a data set using both a measure of center and a measure of spread rather than just one or the other?

4 Once you collect data to answer questions, you will want to decide what measures of center and spread can be used to describe your data.

    a. One student said she could use only the mode to describe categorical data, but that she could use the mode, median, and mean to describe numerical data. Is she right? Explain why or why not.

    b. Can you determine a measure of spread for categorical data? Explain.

Think about your answers to these questions, discuss your ideas with other students and your teacher, and then write a summary of your findings in your journal.

You will soon be developing your own survey to gather information about middle-school students. What measures of center and spread can you use to describe the data you might collect for each question in your survey?

Is Anyone Typical?

You can use what you have learned in *Data About Us* to conduct a statistical investigation to answer the question, "What are some characteristics of a typical middle-school student?" When you have completed your investigation, make a poster, write a report, or find some other way to communicate your results.

Your statistical investigation should consist of four parts:

Posing questions
You will want to gather both numerical data and categorical data. Your data may include physical characteristics, family characteristics, miscellaneous behavior (such as hobbies), and preferences or opinions. Once you have decided what you want to know, you need to write appropriate questions. Make sure that your questions are clear so that everyone who takes your survey will interpret them in the same way.

Collecting the data
You may want to collect data from just your class or from a larger group of students. You also need to decide how to distribute and collect the survey.

Analyzing the data
Once you have collected your data, you need to organize, display, and analyze them. Be sure to think about what kinds of displays and which measures of center are most appropriate for each set of data values you collect.

Interpreting the results
Use the results of your analysis to describe some characteristics of the typical middle-school student. Is there a student that fits all the "typical" characteristics you found? If not, explain why.

Looking Back and Looking Ahead

Unit Reflections

Working on the problems in this unit, you explored some of the big ideas involved in conducting statistical investigations. You learned how to represent data using *bar graphs, line plots, stem-and-leaf plots*, and *coordinate graphs*. You explored ways of using statistics such as the *mean*, the *median*, and the *range* to answer questions about data such as "What's typical?" Finally, you developed a variety of ways to compare data sets.

Using Your Statistical Reasoning—Statistical reasoning is often used by naturalists in studies of wild animal population. For example, data in the following table show the lengths (in inches) and weights (in pounds) of 25 alligators captured in central Florida. Aerial photographs give data about the numbers and locations of other wild alligators. It is possible to estimate alligator length from photographs; it is harder to estimate weight.

1 *Consider the lengths of the alligators in the sample.*

a. Make a graph of the lengths of the 25 alligators and write a sentence describing the distribution of lengths shown in the graph.

Lengths and Weights of Captured Alligators						
Gator Number	Length (inches)	Weight (pounds)		Gator Number	Length (inches)	Weight (pounds)
1	74	54		14	88	70
2	94	110		15	58	28
3	85	84		16	90	102
4	61	44		17	94	130
5	128	366		18	68	39
6	72	61		19	78	57
7	89	84		20	86	80
8	90	106		21	72	38
9	63	33		22	74	51
10	82	80		23	147	640
11	114	197		24	76	42
12	69	36		25	86	90
13	86	83				

b. What are the mean and median lengths?   **c.** What is the range of the lengths?

2 *Consider the weights of alligators in the sample.*

    a. Make a graph of the weights of the 25 alligators and write a sentence describing the distribution of weights shown in the graph.

    b. What are the mean and median weights?

    c. What is the range of the weights?

3 *Explore the relationship between the length and weight of Florida alligators.*

    a. Make a coordinate graph of the (length, weight) data.

    b. What relationship do you notice between length and weight of alligators that are

      i. 61 and 63 inches long?   **ii.** 82, 85, and 86 inches long?

      iii. 90, 94, and 114 inches long?

    c. What weight would you predict for an alligator that is

      i. 70 inches long?   **ii.** 100 inches long?   **iii.** 130 inches long?

    d. Based on your study of the alligator length and weight data, do you believe it is possible to make a good estimate for the weight of an alligator if you know its length?

Explaining Your Reasoning—When you describe a collection of data, you look for the shape of the distribution of the data. You can often visualize data patterns using graphs.

1. How do the *mean* and the *median* help in describing the numbers in a data set?

2. How does the *range* help in describing the numbers in a data set?

3. What kinds of numerical data are best displayed with

    a. line plots?   **b.** stem-and-leaf plots?   **c.** coordinate graphs?

4. What does it mean to say that a person's armspan *is related to* his or her height, or that the time it takes to travel to school *is related to* the distance traveled, or that the weight of an alligator *is related to* its length?

The ideas about numerical and graphic data analysis that you have learned in this unit will be used and extended in a variety of future *Connected Mathematics* units, especially Samples and Populations where you will collect, organize, and display numerical information. You'll also find that various statistical plots and data summaries appear in everyday news reports and in the technical work of science, business, and government.

Glossary

axis, axes The number lines that are used to make a graph. There are usually two axes perpendicular to each other (see *bar graphs* or *coordinate graphs* for examples). The vertical axis is called the *y*-axis and the horizontal axis is called the *x*-axis.

bar graph (bar chart) A graphical representation of a table of data in which the height of each bar indicates its value. The bars are separated from each other to highlight that the data are discrete or "counted" data. The horizontal axis shows the values or categories and the vertical axis shows the frequency or tally for each of the values or categories on the horizontal axis.

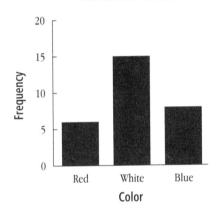

Favorite Colors

categorical data Values that are "words" that represent possible responses within a given category. Frequency counts can be made of the values for a given category. See the examples that follow.

- Months of the year in which people have birthdays (values may be January, February, March, and so on)
- Favorite color to wear for a t-shirt (values may be magenta, Carolina blue, yellow, and so on)
- Kinds of pets people have (values may be cats, dogs, fish, horses, boa constrictors, and so on)

coordinate graph A graphical representation of pairs of related numerical values. One axis shows one value of each pair (for example, height on the horizontal axis) and the other axis shows the other value of each pair (for example, arm span on the vertical axis). The graph below shows a coordinate graph of the data in the table.

Measures (inches)

Initials	Height	Arm Span
JJ	69	67
NY	63	60
CM	73	75
PL	77	77

Height and Arm Span Measurements

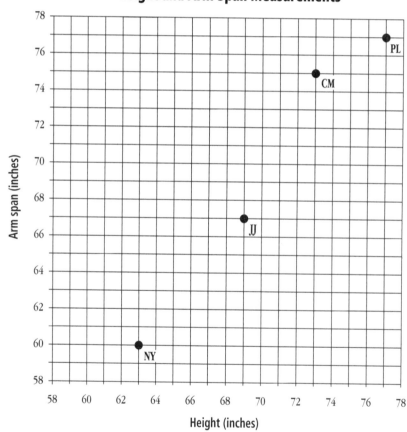

data Values such as counts, ratings, measurements, or opinions that are gathered to answer questions. The data in this table show mean temperatures in three cities.

Daily Mean Temperatures

City	Mean Temperature
Mobile, AL	67.5 °F
Boston, MA	51.3 °F
Spokane, WA	47.3 °F

line plot A quick, simple way to organize data along a number line where the Xs (or other symbols) above a number represent how often each value is mentioned.

Numbers of Siblings Students Have

```
              X
  X     X  X        X
  X  X  X  X  X  X
  X  X  X  X  X  X  X        X
 ─────────────────────────────
  0  1  2  3  4  5  6  7  8
```
Number of siblings

mean A value that represents a middle value or typical value in a set of data. If all the data had the same value, the mean would be that value. For example, the total number of siblings for the above data is 56 siblings. If all 19 students had the same number of siblings, they would each have about 3 siblings.

median The numerical value that marks the middle of an ordered set of data. Half the data occur above the median, and half the data occur below the median. The median of the distribution of siblings is 3 because the tenth (middle) value in the ordered set of 19 values (0, 0, 0, 1, 1, 2, 2, 2, 2, 3, 3, 3, 4, 4, 5, 5, 5, 6, 8) is 3 siblings.

mode Of a distribution, the category or numerical value that occurs most often. For example, the mode of the distribution of the number of siblings is 2. It is possible for a set of data to have more than one mode.

numerical data Values that are numbers such as counts, measurements, and ratings. As an example, see *data* and the examples that follow.

- Numbers of children in families
- Pulse rates indicating how many heart beats occur in a minute
- Height
- How much time people spend reading in one day
- How much people value something, such as: On a scale of 1 to 5 with 1 as "low interest," how would you rate your interest in participating in the school's field day?

outlier One or more values that lie "outside" of a distribution of the data. An outlier is a value that may be questioned because it is unusual or because there may have been an error in recording or reporting the data.

range The range of a distribution is computed by stating the lowest and highest values. For example, the range of the number of siblings is from 0 to 8 people.

scale The size of the units on an axis of a graph or number line. For instance, each mark on the vertical axis might represent 10 units.

stem-and-leaf plot (stem plot) A quick way to picture the shape of a distribution while including the actual numerical values in the graph. For a number like 25, the stem 2 is written at the left of the vertical line, and the leaf, 5, is at the right.

Numbers of Movies Seen Over the Summer

```
0 |
1 | 5 5 5 5
2 | 2 5 0
3 | 0 5
4 |
5 |
6 | 0
```

Back-to-back stem plots may be used to compare two sets of the same kind of data. The units for one set of data are placed on one side of the stem, and the units for the other set are placed on the other side.

survey A method for collecting data that uses interviews. Surveys ask questions to find out information such as facts, opinions, or beliefs.

Favorite Colors

Color	Number of Students
Red	6
White	15
Blue	9

table A tool for organizing information in rows and columns. Tables let you list categories or values and then tally the occurrences. For an example, see *data*.

datos Valores como cómputos, calificaciones, medidas u opiniones que se recogen para responder preguntas. Los datos en esta tabla representan las temperaturas medias en tres ciudades.

Temperaturas medias diarias

Ciudad	Temp. media
Mobile, AL	67.5 °F
Boston, MA	51.3 °F
Spokane, WA	47.3 °F

datos categóricos Valores que son "palabras" que representan posibles respuestas en una categoría dada. Se pueden contar las frecuencias de los valores para una categoría dada. Observa los ejemplos siguientes:

- Los meses del año en los que las personas cumplen años (los valores pueden ser enero, febrero, marzo y así sucesivamente)
- El color favorito para una camiseta (los valores pueden ser púrpura, azul Carolina, amarillo y así sucesivamente)
- Los tipos de mascotas que tienen las personas (los valores pueden ser gatos, perros, peces, caballos, boas constrictores y así sucesivamente)

datos numéricos Valores que son números como, por ejemplo, cómputos, medidas y calificaciones. Observa el ejemplo que se da en *datos* y en los siguientes ejemplos.

- Número de hijos e hijas en las familias
- Frecuencia del pulso que indica cuántas veces late el corazón en un minuto
- Altura
- La cantidad de tiempo que las personas leen en un día
- El valor que las personas le dan a algo, como por ejemplo: "En una escala de 1 a 5, en la que 1 representa "poco interés", ¿cómo calificarías tu interés por participar en el día de campo de tu escuela?"

diagrama de puntos Una manera rápida y sencilla de organizar datos en una recta numérica donde las X (u otros símbolos) colocadas encima de un número representan la frecuencia con que se menciona cada valor.

Números de hermanos y hermanas que tienen los estudiantes

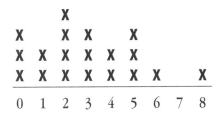

Número de hermanos y hermanas

ejes Las rectas numéricas que se usan para hacer una gráfica. Generalmente hay dos ejes perpendiculares uno a otro. (*Véase gráficas de barras* o *gráficas de coordenadas*.) El eje vertical se llama eje de las *y* y el eje horizontal se llama eje de las *x*.

encuesta Un método para recoger datos que utiliza entrevistas. En las encuestas se hacen preguntas para averiguar información tal como hechos, opiniones o creencias.

Colores favoritos

Color	Número de estudiantes
Rojo	6
Blanco	15
Azul	9

escala El tamaño de la unidad en un eje de una gráfica o recta numérica. Por ejemplo, cada marca en el eje vertical puede representar 10 unidades.

gama La gama de una distribución se calcula determinando los valores mínimo y máximo. Por ejemplo, la gama del número de hermanos y hermanas es de 0 a 8 personas.

gráfica de barras Representación gráfica de una tabla de datos en la que la altura de cada barra indica su valor. Las barras están separadas entre sí para subrayar que los datos son discretos o "contados". El eje horizontal representa los valores o categorías y el eje vertical representa la frecuencia o el cómputo de cada uno de los valores o categorías en el eje horizontal.

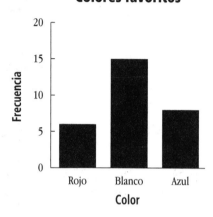

gráfica de coordenadas Una representación gráfica de pares de valores numéricos relacionados. Un eje representa un valor de cada par (por ejemplo, la altura de una persona en el eje horizontal) y el otro eje representa el otro valor de cada par (por ejemplo, el largo de los brazos abiertos en el eje vertical). La gráfica siguiente representa una gráfica de coordenadas de los datos de la tabla.

Medidas (pulgadas)

Iniciales	Altura	Largo de los brazos abiertos
JJ	69	67
NY	63	60
CM	73	75
PL	77	77

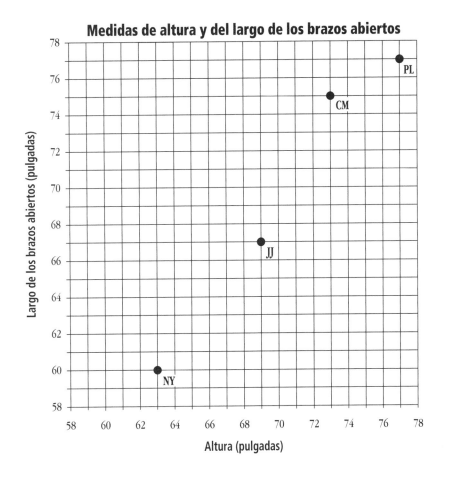

Medidas de altura y del largo de los brazos abiertos

media Un valor que representa un valor medio o un valor típico en un conjunto de datos. Si todos los datos tuvieran el mismo valor, la media sería ese valor. Por ejemplo, el número total de hermanos y hermanas para los datos en el diagrama de puntos es de 56. Si los 19 estudiantes tuvieran la misma cantidad de hermanos y hermanas, cada uno tendría aproximadamente 3 hermanos o hermanas.

mediana El valor numérico que señala la mitad en un conjunto ordenado de datos. La mitad de los datos ocurre encima de la mediana y la otra mitad de los datos ocurre debajo de la mediana. La mediana de la distribución de hermanos y hermanas es 3 porque el décimo valor (el del medio) en el conjunto ordenado de 19 valores (0, 0, 0, 1, 1, 2, 2, 2, 2, 3, 3, 3, 4, 4, 5, 5, 5, 6, 8) es 3 hermanos o hermanas.

modo En una distribución es la categoría o el valor numérico lo que ocurre con mayor frecuencia. Por ejemplo, el modo de la distribución del número de hermanos o hermanas es 2. Es posible que un conjunto de datos tenga más de un modo.

tabla Una herramienta para organizar información en filas y columnas. Las tablas permiten que se hagan listas de categorías o de valores y luego se computen las ocurrencias. Para un ejemplo, ver *datos*.

tabla arborescente (tallo y hojas) Una manera rápida y sencilla de hacer un dibujo con la forma de una distribución y al mismo tiempo incluir los valores numéricos reales en la gráfica. Para un número como 25, el tallo 2 se escribe a la izquierda de la línea vertical, y la hoja 5, a la derecha de la línea.

Números de películas vistas durante el verano

```
0 |
1 | 5  5  5  5
2 | 2  5  0
3 | 0  5
4 |
5 |
6 | 0
```

Las tablas arborescentes compuestas pueden usarse para comparar dos conjuntos del mismo tipo de datos. Las unidades de un conjunto de datos se ponen de un lado del tallo y las unidades del otro conjunto se ponen en el otro lado.

valor extremo Uno o más valores que caen "afuera" de una distribución de los datos. El valor extremo es un valor que puede ser cuestionado porque está fuera de lo normal o porque puede haber ocurrido un error al registrar o informar los datos.

Index